D0095832

Every Decision You Make Is a Spiritual One

Anthony J. De Conciliis, C.S.C.
with
John F. Kinsella

Paulist Press
New York/Mahwah, New Jersey

Dedication

The People of St. Francis of Assisi Mission, A Growing Community

Cover/book design and interior illustrations by Nicholas T. Markell.

Copyright © 1995 by Anthony J. De Conciliis, C.S.C.

All rights reserved. No part of this book may be reproduced or transmitted in any form or by any means, electronic or mechanical, including photocopying, recording or by any information storage and retrieval system without permission in writing from the Publisher.

Library of Congress Cataloging-in-Publication Data

De Conciliis, Anthony, 1941-
    Every decision you make is a spiritual one / Anthony J. De Concilliis with John F. Kinsella.
        p.   cm.— (IlluminationBooks)
    Includes bibliographical references (p.).
    ISBN 0-8091-3562-0 (alk. paper)
    1. Spiritual life—Christianity. 2. Decision-making—Religious aspects—Christianity. I. Kinsella, John F. II. Title. III. Series.
BV4501.2.D414   1995
248.4—dc20   95-2309
                                                    CIP

Published by Paulist Press
997 Macarthur Boulevard
Mahwah, New Jersey 07430

Printed and bound in the
United States of America

Contents

IlluminationBooks

A Foreword

*I*lluminationBooks bring to light wonderful ideas, helpful information, and sound spirituality in concise, illustrative, readable, and eminently practical works on topics of current concern. Learning from stress; interior peace; personal prayer; biblical awareness; walking with others in darkness; appreciating the love already in our lives; spiritual discernment; uncovering helpful psychological antidotes for our tendency to worry too much at times; and important guides to improving interpersonal relations, are only several of the areas which will be covered in this series.

The goal of each IlluminationBook, then, is to provide great ideas, helpful steps, and needed inspiration in small volumes. Each book offers a new beginning for the reader to explore possibilities and embrace practicalities which can be employed in everyday life.

In today's busy and anxious world, Illumination-Books are meant to provide a source of support—without requiring an inordinate amount of time or prior preparation. Each small work stands on its own. Hopefully, the information provided not only will be nourishing in itself but also will encourage further exploration in the area.

One is obviously never done learning. With every morsel of wisdom each of these books provides, the goal is to keep the process of seeking knowledge ongoing even during busy times, when sitting down with a larger work is impossible or undesirable.

However, more than information (as valuable as it is), at the base of each work in the series is a deep sense of *hope* that is based on a belief in the beautiful statement made by Jesus to his disciples and in turn to us: "You are my friends" (Jn 15:15).

As "friends of God" we must seek the presence of the Lord in ourselves, in others, in silence and solitude, in nature, and in daily situations. IlluminationBooks are designed to provide implicit and explicit opportunities to appreciate this reality in new ways. So, it is in this spirit that this book and the other ones in the series are offered to you.   —*Robert J. Wicks*

General Editor, IlluminationBooks

Introduction
The Spirit of Life and Decisions

*T*he development of your spiritual life, empowered by the Spirit of God, is a major decision in your life. In St. Paul's sensitive lesson to the Romans—and to us—about spirituality, the Christian's spiritual life, he contrasted the order of sin and death with the new order of the Holy Spirit. "The reason, therefore, why those who are in Christ Jesus are not condemned is that the law of the spirit of life in Christ Jesus has set you free from the law of sin and death" (Rom 8:1–2). For him, the word spirit, in "spirit of life," means "either the Holy Spirit in person or the spirit of man (humanity) made new by his presence."[1] The basic message is that the person who intentionally decides to accept Jesus is empowered by the Spirit of God. The development of a spirit of life, a spirituality, is based primarily on an active and deep relationship with the Son of God. St. Paul reminds us that "God has done what the Law, because of our unspiritual nature, was unable to do" (Rom 8:3). Of course, he is referring to what Jesus did for us; that is, we are made spiritual through union with him.

St. Paul emphasizes in Romans 8:5 that the possession of a spirit of life demands a real decision to be interested in spiritual things (things of the Spirit) rather than unspiritual things (things of the flesh). Biblical scholar Joseph Fitzmyer translates this verse about unspiritual things in this way: "Those who live according to the flesh are concerned about things of the flesh, i.e., those whose motivation in life is a self-centered interest; their aspirations are self-oriented."[2] Fitzmyer suggests that "living according to the flesh" concerns an outlook on life or a mindset or a way of thinking and desiring. This person does not care for God or others but only for the self. Those whose interests limit them to the unspiritual (flesh), the order of sin and death (in contrast to the new order of the Holy Spirit), are "at enmity with God" and "such a limitation never could and never does submit to God's law" (Rom 8:5–8).

Paul goes on to say that if we choose (or decide) to be concerned about the spiritual, we choose life and peace (Rom 8:6), that is, life and friendship with God. He teaches that when we make a decision to be a believer in Jesus, we begin to develop a spirit of life characterized by reconciliation and peace with God. Finally, in verses 10–11, he summarizes the core of Jesus' message, the core of Christian spirituality:

> Though your body may be dead it is because of sin, but if Christ is in you then your spirit is life itself because you have been justified; and if the Spirit of him who raised Jesus from the dead is living in you, then he who raised Jesus from the dead will give life to your own mortal bodies through his Spirit living in you.

A Christian spirituality, then, has as its foundation the belief in the work of Jesus through his passion, death and resurrection and a committed decision to live in God's Spirit.

Spirituality explored

There have been many definitions suggested for the word spirituality. Author and professor Bernard McGinn, when speaking about spirituality as an academic discipline, has said, "Spirituality...usually has to rely on the fickleness of academics to try to speak its name, though this fact has never prevented people from just doing it and not bothering about defining it."[3] McGinn summarizes the many definitions of spirituality in his article. In the twelfth century, the noun, *spiritualitas*, was used to signify a power animating Christian life and a

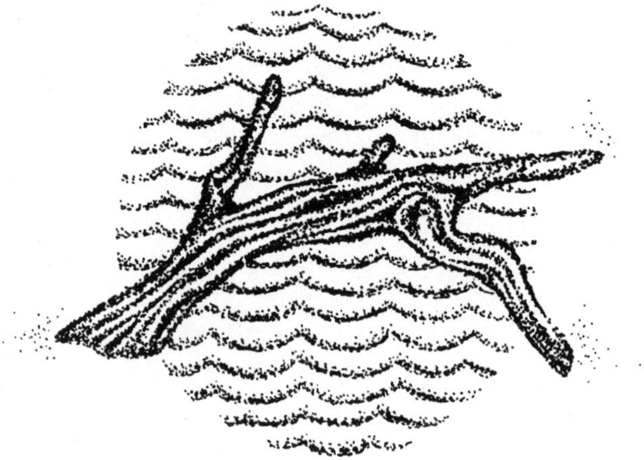

power which pertains to the soul. At the beginning of the sixteenth century, the Latin adjective, *spirituale*, referred to "the whole person's way of acting." In the later part of the sixteenth century and in the seventeenth century, the term, spirituality, signified the inner dispositions or the interior states of the soul. As a consequence, the terms "devotion" and "piety" became popular for both Catholics and Protestants. McGinn believes that today the majority of definitions "can be described as variants of 'anthropological' understandings, that is, ones that put the greatest stress on spirituality as an element in human nature and experience."[4] Many of the modern definitions include concepts such as human authenticity, transcendence, self-transcendence, and the lived experience of the person.

In practical terms, many view spirituality as an inward attitude which influences our daily experiences, that is, a way of living. Others suggest that spirituality can be viewed in a simpler way. John Garvey,[5] for example, understands spirituality as a process of staying awake when you desperately want to fall asleep. It is a process of discovery, an awareness. He gives this intriguing analogy about the spiritual life:

> The spiritual life is a process something like erosion, or something like the way driftwood is formed by the passing current. Our process in it, apart from the struggle, may be limited to a present awareness of what the alternative is: not to be formed, or to think of the self as autonomous.

While his analogy about the spiritual life may be too passive for some in that all we need do is to pay attention and allow God to form us, he does point out that the spiritual life is a process of formation in which we remain awake and willing to discover. Moreover, he admits that there is a struggle in the process of discovery.

Another writer who describes spirituality of everyday life is Gerald Broccolo. He believes that "...the most accurate definition of spirituality is simply 'how I cope with life.'"[6] His definition includes two components: a way of viewing the world (attitude) and a way of experiencing life (behavior). This way of viewing the concept of spirituality embraces each and every human being. If this is true, then it stands to reason that everyone who is alive has a spirituality, even the professed atheist. But surely, spirituality is more than a psychosocial complex geared to deal with everyday life. Ultimately, a definition of spirituality must include a reference to the transcendent. Broccolo says that what makes coping with life a Christian experience is our participation in the Christ of faith. For example, Christian liturgy integrates the mystery of Jesus, the dying and rising experience of Jesus, into the dying and rising experience of people's daily life.

Another way to understand the nature of spirituality is to view it as an expression of the heart's yearnings. Spirituality is the expression of what our hearts draw us to. Each decision, honestly made, draws a person closer to his or her heart—which ultimately draws each to the mystery of God.

Facing the mystery of God rather than hiding from the mystery is the goal of a healthy spirituality. Therefore, it is a heart-searching process, just as Martin Buber suggested: "Everyone should carefully observe what way his heart draws him to, and then choose the way with all his strength."[7] This heart-searching process is unique to each person since it is developed within each one's heart. Buber said, "Every man's foremost task is the actualization of his unique, unprecedented and never-recurring potentialities, and not the repetition of something that another, and be it even the greatest, has already achieved."[8]

In this book, the major challenge was to accept a definition or description of spirituality that related to the decision-making and the spiritual life. In this decision-making process, the following definitions were considered:

- Spirituality is not something we do; it is more properly our way of daily living.
- Spirituality is not a way of predicting what will happen in life; it is a way of viewing and interpreting life in the present.
- Spirituality is not a concrete blueprint; it is a vision for life that puts the spiritual life above all.
- Spirituality is not a corpus of beliefs or a creed; it is a way of believing that makes sense to the person.
- Spirituality is not something we decide to do; it is the filter through which we decide what we ought to do.
- Spirituality does not describe what we will become; it presents a vision of who we are.

After all these considerations, this conclusion emerged: spirituality can be best described as the spirit of life. This spirit of life is ongoing and is the product of the many decisions of life, from the beginning to the end of life on earth. This spirit of life, the spiritual center, is the filter for all our human experiences. It inspires action through decision and makes possible our individual discoveries about the mystery of life.

Decisions and the spirit of life

The clear relationship between a person's spirit of life and day-to-day decisions almost dictated the title of this book. Because it is impossible to examine all the decisions of life, however, we will focus on five major decisions and their dependence on the spirit of life.

These decisions mirror and impact on the many decisions that we make each day at home, at school, at work, at play, in friendships, in conversations, in commitments, in marriage, in business, and most especially, in relationship to God in the quiet of our hearts. They are basic in helping one to develop a healthy spiritual life. Of course, they do not exhaust the extensive pool of critical decisions that might be considered as part of life, but they may prompt you to consider others that play a significant role in your spiritual life.

The following five decisions discussed in this book represent, in a broad way, the outline of normal development. We will look at each of these decisions as part of our everyday spiritual life. They are:

The Decision to Believe
The Decision to Love
The Decision to Work
The Decision to Endure
The Decision to Serve.

*   *   *

Let's consider the following as a starting point in our thinking about each person's spirit of life and decisions:

The stuff of living a healthy life is the stuff of the developing of one's spiritual life. Every decision becomes a spiritual one because it is automatically filtered through one's spirit of life (spirituality) which is based on the acceptance of the Spirit of God in the heart and soul.

Chapter One
Decision-Making and the Spiritual Life

*T*he ability to make decisions is a fundamental human process in developing and maintaining a healthy psychological and spiritual life. Because of the important role that decision-making plays in a person's cognitive and emotional life, many philosophers, theologians, and psychologists have discussed it over the centuries. Experiential findings and commonsense thinking about the nature of decisions and decision-making tell us the following:

• One decision can dramatically affect the course of a life. This type of decision may be automatic, such as an instantaneous decision while operating a vehicle which causes an injury or death to another, or a deliberate, intentional decision such as drinking to excess to deal with stress in a marriage or other relationship.

• One decision can serve as the basis for many other decisions. William James, in his classic book, *The Varieties of Religious Experience*, suggests that there are three fundamental, self-seeking, instinctive impulses in the development of the self: bodily, social, and spiritual. True spiritual self-seeking for him is "the search of the redeemed inward nature, the spotlessness from sin, whether here or hereafter...."[9] He continues by saying that the preservation of the spiritual self is "so supremely precious that, rather than lose it, a man ought to be willing to give up friends and good fame, and property...."[10] Vincent Foster, a former attorney and legal counselor for President Clinton, said to law students just before his death by suicide: "Following the bar exam, your most difficult test will not be what you know but what is your character. Some of you will fail...there is no victory, no advantage, no fee, no favor which is worth even a blemish on your reputation."[11] Vincent Foster counsels us to value achievement, but achievement in life that is tempered by the decision to preserve the spiritual self.

• Good decision-making is an important factor in the development of a healthy and hardy life-style. Robert Lifton, who is known for his research and writing on the survivors of Nazi death camp doctors, suggests that humans are resilient even in the face of political, social, and moral confusion. He says that "...we have been evolving a sense of self appropriate to the restlessness and flux of our time. This mode of being...enables us to engage in continuous exploration and personal experiment."[12] The "Protean Self" is the name he gives to this emerging and resilient self, an allusion to the Greek god Proteus, who was able to change shape in the face of crisis.

In life, decisions have to be faced. "Should I seek the position or not?" "Is it the best salary that I can get for that job?" "Is that person the best marriage partner for me?" "Do I really believe in God?" "Can I ever stop drinking?" "Is that an ethical decision?" "Should I minister to the needs of the needy?" "Is this act immoral?"

Spiritual decisions

William James was intrigued with the issue of decision-making and the role of the will or a "feeling of effort," in the process of a "deliberate action." Many of our routine decisions are made almost automatically each day; for example, the route to take to work, what to have for dinner, or the choice of a racquetball partner. But for James, more important decisions—including spiritual decisions—must have that "feeling of effort."[13] In this type of decision-making, a higher motive—one that is moral and spiritual—is involved. The decisions made by the rescuers of the Jews,[14] and the interventions made by bystanders during emergencies[15] are examples of this type of decision-making.

In his creative and innovative chapter on the will, William James presents a very insightful discussion on the decision-making process. He believed that significant decisions demand creative intentions that are informed by reason or by a creative contribution (a spiritual phenomenon). In his theory, there are five types of decision, each moving toward a more intentional experience. The first four types include various levels of decision-making beginning with almost total passivity. In the first type, "the reasonable type," the person waits until the decision is made as a result of the natural course of things. By contrast, in the fourth type, the person's decisions and deliberations are affected by something outside, like a "change of heart" or "awakenings of conscience," such as a natural disaster or the loss of a loved one. The fifth type, however, is a highly developed process which includes an active deliberation process that is important for the spiritual life.

In the fifth type, the person is "involved in the decision" since it is a willful act. The "feeling of effort" is present unlike the other types of decision-making. Whether the decision was accomplished by reasoning or a creative contribution of something other than reason (the work of the Holy Spirit), the person makes a deliberate choice, "an excursion into a lonesome moral wilderness."[16]

James describes this decision-making process as "driving a thorn into one's flesh" because the person realizes, after carefully entertaining the possibilities and keeping aware of them, how much would be lost by choosing one over the other, that is, spiritual things over unspiritual

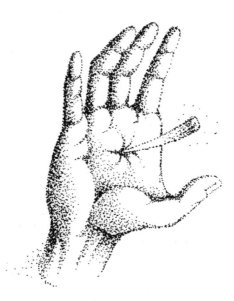

things as described by St. Paul. James and St. Paul may be suggesting a spiritual decision-making process. There are numerous examples of this type of process. A person may be moved to action by the plight of an individual or a group of people. The decision may result from the combination of personal moral development and reflection on the circumstances of the present moment. In our modern day, the charitable work of Danny Thomas and Jerry Lewis on behalf of suffering children serves as a good example. One cannot but be moved by Lewis' dedication, year after year, to raise consciousness and money for "his kids."

There is no doubt that there are many factors that are involved in a spiritual or moral decision-making process. Andrew Garrod suggests that the study of moral development has become a very important topic for academic research. He says, "The only real question is perhaps the most basic one: What does 'moral development' mean to all the diversity of scholars who have become interested in it?" He goes on to say that "It is clear from the start that there are multiple answers to this question. Rather than a single construct, the answer is a loose constellation of ideas...."[17] What spiritual development is may be very similar to the process of moral development throughout the life span. Thus spiritual development may be a constellation of decisions characterized by the "feeling of effort," something accomplished by reasoning or a creative contribution of something other than reason (the work of the Holy Spirit). Perhaps spiritual development is a decision-making process where there is "an excursion into a lonesome moral wilderness."

*   *   *

This book suggests five basic decisions—excursions into the wilderness, if you will—which seem to be common to each person's development through life. Consider these five basic decisions as important points in the development of a spiritual life.

Chapter Two
The Decision to Believe

*T*he decision to believe does not usually result from a lightning-bolt experience. It is a process, developed over a series of years and experiences which are really experiences of revelation about ourselves and others in relationship to our God, the transcendent one. The decision to believe is the foundation for our spiritual life.

The scriptures are filled with examples of the decision to believe. One very graphic story tells about Peter's decision to walk on water based on his newly discovered ability to act on his belief (Mt 14:22–33). Peter, amazed by the power of Jesus even over the basic elements, decided to show that his decision to believe was not merely words without potential for action. Almost out of impulse, he said, "...tell me to come across the water." But, he did not focus his attention on Jesus and so his fear overcame him. Perhaps his decision to believe was not fully mature. Nevertheless, the experience helped him to discover something new about himself. This experience was added to all the other discoveries and helped form his spiritual life. His decision helped him to take chances, even when his own well-being was at stake. His decision to walk on the water was a spiritual one. It brought him to a clearer decision about his belief and his own values.

At the end of his letter to the Philippians, St. Paul took the opportunity to remind them of his decision to believe. The Philippians had expressed their concern for St. Paul. He responded in a very sensitive way by explaining that he had experienced many joys and hardships. "I have been through my initiation and now I am ready for anything anywhere: full stomach or empty stomach, poverty or plenty. There is nothing I cannot master with the help of the One who gives me strength" (Phil 4:12–13). In this way, he affirmed that his decision to believe in Christ underlined his commitment to others.

The struggle to believe and the spiritual life

Each one of us struggles with the decision to believe. Nikos Kazantzakis, the famous author of *Zorba the Greek*, spent many years of his life writing a book, *The Saviors of God: Spiritual Exercises*, which outlined his decision to believe. At one point in the book he says this about his own belief struggle: "I have one longing only: to grasp what is hidden behind appearances, to ferret out that mystery which brings me to birth and then kills me, to discover if behind the visible and unceasing stream of the world an invisible and immutable presence is hiding."[18] Kazantzakis' decision to believe became a lifelong struggle. He desired to find peace in a deeper reason to believe, a type of faith-state. At one point in his reflection on the decision to believe, he said:

> A command rings out within me: Dig! What do you see? Men and birds, water and stones.
>
> Dig deeper! What do you see? Ideas and dreams, fantasies and lightning flashes! Dig deeper! What do you see? I see nothing! A mute Night, as thick as death. It must be death. Dig deeper! Ah! I cannot penetrate the dark partition!
>
> Beyond the mind, on the edge of the heart's holy precipice, I proceed, trembling.
>
> Behind all appearances, I divine a struggling essence, I want to merge with it.
>
> I feel that behind appearances this struggling essence is also striving to merge with my heart.[19]

These words express a desire to understand the essence of life or the intimate relationship between a sense of immanence and transcendence. It is a perplexing struggle that

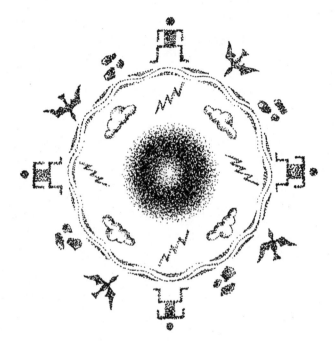

all of us, at one time or another, undergo—"Is that all there is to life?" This type of questioning is most apparent in late adulthood. After each person has resolved (to the best of his or her ability) the normal childhood and young adulthood passages, such as Autonomy, Industry, Identity, and Intimacy, the time comes to resolve those issues which relate to the meaning and belief values, such as Generativity and Integrity. Erikson says that these latter life developmental stages concern the establishment and the guidance of the next generation; expansion of the ego's interests; "ultimate concerns," such as the care for others and the world; an experience of charity toward others; and an acceptance of "one's one and only life cycle as something that had to be and that, by necessity, permitted of no substitutions."[20] He says that a person who develops a style of Integrity through culture or civilization experiences the final consolation: death losing its sting. The decision is part of the process of life.

Psychology and belief

William James, one of the celebrated names in psychology, was a great advocate of investigating belief and religious experience. In his books, *Principles of Psychology* and *Varieties of Religious Experience*, he investigates the nature of belief and its role in the person. For example, in *Principles* he says that belief is not only apprehended by the mind, an experience of the imagination, but it is also based in reality. Belief, for him, is a feeling which is more connected to the emotions than to anything else.

He, like many other scientists, struggled with the "decision to believe." In *Principles*, he proposes several theories for the development of consciousness—among them the Soul-Theory, a revolutionary idea for a scientist of his time to consider. While James could not completely support this as the major theory for the conception of the consciousness, he confessed that he had to consider it. He said:

> But the plain fact is that all the arguments...[theories for the conception of states of consciousness] are also arguments for that well-known spiritual agent in which scholastic psychology and common-sense have always believed. The fact is that one cannot afford to despise any of these great traditional objects of belief.[21]

James was convinced that there was an interaction between body and soul, and was one of the first to express his doubt in the finality of pure mechanistic or rationalistic methods to explain consciousness in the human person.[22] In a very characteristic way, he expresses his ideas about scientific enlightenment and the efficacy of prayer when speaking about the development of the social self:

> We hear, in these days of scientific enlightenment, a great deal of discussion about the efficacy of prayer; and many reasons are given us why we should not pray, whilst others are given us why we should. But in all this very little is said of the reason why we do pray, which is simply that we can-

not help praying. It seems probable that, in spite of all that "science" may do to the contrary, men will continue to pray to the end of time, unless their mental nature changes in a manner which nothing we know should lead us to expect.[23]

William James and the decision to believe

In *The Varieties of Religious Experience* James presents his strongest arguments for the influence of worldviews, spirituality, and beliefs on human development. Based on the reported sentiments of religious people, the searchings of their hearts, he pointed out how decisions to believe influenced the course of lives. For example, one of the testimonies came from a woman who was not taught Christian doctrine, but simply made it a practice to read the Bible and to pray. She said, "To this day, I cannot understand dallying with religion and the commands of God. The very instant I heard my Father's cry calling unto me, my heart bounded in recognition....The idea of God's reality has never left me for one moment."[24]

Another example of a person who experienced the overwhelming presence of God came from a forty-nine-year-old man. James commented that "...probably thousands of unpretending Christians would write an almost identical account."[25] The person said:

> God is more real to me than any thought or thing or person....I talk to him as to a companion in prayer and praise, and our communion is delight-

ful. He answers me again and again, often in words so clearly spoken that it seems my outer ear must have carried the tone, but generally in strong mental impressions. Usually, a text of Scripture, unfolding some new view of him and his love for me, and care for my safety. I could give hundreds of instances, in school matters, social problems, financial difficulties, etc. That he is mine and I am his never leaves me, it is an abiding joy.[26]

This person's decisions were filtered through his spirituality; his spirituality literally enfolded his entire life—school, social and financial. His day-to-day experiences speak of his partnership with a reality of love and care. When defending the reality of these mystical experiences, James, probably addressing his comments to an audience schooled in rationalism, suggested that those who had these feelings of reality regard them as perceptions of truth, as revelations.

Everyday examples of the decision to believe

If we but only listen to people whose words and actions express their spirituality, we discover many examples of the decision to believe.

Bob is a professor of biology with a specialty in the study of plants. For years he could not assent to the reality of a living and vital God who would care to interact in his life course. "It is not that I did not believe in God, but I just did not think that this transcendent God related personally to me and my world." In the last five years, this has all changed for him. "I don't know when it happened exactly, but gradually I came to the realization that I could have a personal relationship with God. Now I know that he is close to me as I make decisions." He revealed that his attitude had been one of a rationalistic nature. He could not explain this personal relationship on an experiential level, so it did not exist. When he decided to be open to another plane of existence, one that could not be explained merely through experience, he changed. In fact, he discovered new facets of his own spirituality. His friends always had attributed Bob's charitable behavior to God's life in him, even though he himself did not realize it. His view of himself changed with his decision to believe.

Harry, an accountant who is married with three children, listens intently for the urgings of Jesus and Mary to help him make decisions in his everyday life. Each day, he gets up at 5:00 a.m. to pray, using the scriptures. Then at 7:00 a.m., he attends the eucharist with his wife and one of his children. An extraordinary experience led him to put his trust in the word of Mary. While dressing one morning, he felt that the Blessed Virgin wanted him to take his family to Medjugorje. It was so clear to him that, after discussing it with his wife who also has a strong devotion to the Virgin Mary, he decided to sell his house. This gave them the capital to take the trip. His decision to believe included this expression of obedience. He claimed that he felt a sense of calm and peace, even though by nature he had grave uncertainty about financial security.

His life and the lives of his family have been changed dramatically by their visit to Medjugorje and by their willing obedience to the word of God through Mary. This spiritual act brought deeper meaning into their lives.

The heart: imagination and healing

James Hillman[27] says that the heart is the seat of imagination and the residence of the transpersonal. When we confess our need for a more transcendent meaningfulness, our hearts open up to the images of our inner humanness. It is these images which give rise to feelings and, finally, to the decision to believe (or doubt). Moving into the human heart through prayer and reflection enables awareness of and interaction with the ground of being, the holy other, the transcendent.

This decision to believe, to be open to our spiritual selves, is so important that Jung claimed that he never really cured a patient in the second half of life unless, in the course of treatment, that person found access to the *religious function.*

His consideration of this *religious function* led Paul Tillich to conclude that "every spiritual act is an act of meaning...,"[28] that is, every decision is a spiritual decision and becomes part of a religious attitude.

* * *

The decision to believe is a spiritual act. For most, it is born as a result of struggle and an effort of the will. However, when it is born, the decision to believe is a real and sensible experience which affects the core of one's personality. It becomes the foundation for all other decisions in life and describes one's spirit of life, or spirituality.

Closely connected to the decision to believe is the decision to love, the indispensable aspect of spirituality.

Chapter Three

The Decision to Love

*T*he vital attitude of lovers is determined by the habitual sense, by which each is haunted, of the other being in the world. A lover has notoriously this sense of the continuous being of his idol, even when his attention is addressed to other matters and he no longer represents her features. He cannot forget her; she uninterruptedly affects him through and through.[29]

The vital attitude to love in scripture

The vital attitude of human love that James refers to in the opening quote, has its basis in the spirit(ual) life.

St. Paul says, "Everyone moved by the Spirit is a son of God. The spirit you received is...the spirit of sons and daughters....The Spirit himself and our spirit bear united witness that we are children of God" (Rom 8:14-17). By our right as heirs of God, St. Paul says that our love is based on God's love. In imitation of his son, we decide to love one another.

In the same chapter of the letter to the Romans, St. Paul affirms God's decision to love us. It is expressed in his promise that he will always be with us in good times and bad. "Nothing therefore can come between us and the love of Christ, even if we are troubled or worried, or being persecuted, or lacking food or clothes, or being threatened or even attacked" (Rom 8:35-36).

Whether we can accept it or not, all spiritual, material, and intellectual goods will pass away, but unconditional love abides forever. St. Paul tells us that the fragmentary things (temporal) shall vanish away, but the complete (eternal) things shall remain (1 Cor 13:8-12). The fragmentary includes, of course, material things, but surprisingly, it also includes some of the divine gifts of the Holy Spirit, such as prophecy and speaking in tongues. Only love does not disappear and it brings with it the full knowledge to come. This is the knowledge of the truth, face-to-face knowledge. There is only one way to be united fully with another person—through love. This love is not blind, but rather a seeing love which penetrates the heart of God and the hearts of men and women.

Accepting this as a major part of the spirit of life,

we cannot ignore the decision to love. All other decisions are profoundly influenced by this spiritual foundation. The decision to love speaks, not only about our words of love, but also about how we actually express it in our behavior over time. In this way love is dynamic, a word of love is an act of love.

From the scriptures we learn that it is God who loved us first. Indeed, throughout history, it was God's word and behavior that modeled the decision to love for all to imitate.

Psychology and the decision to love

The nature of love has been the subject of research and reflection by many philosophers, psychologists, poets and scores of others. This is because love is one of the most intense human emotions and is shared by most people at some time in life. Of course, the degree of love differs for each person depending on the relationship and the situation. For example, typically a person feels greater love for family and spouse than for casual friends.

In his book, *The Art of Loving*, Erich Fromm distinguishes various types of love, such as brotherly love, motherly love, erotic love, love of God and self-love. For him, self-love (not narcissistic self-indulgence that excludes the love of others which appears to be so prevalent in our day) is most important and the prerequisite for loving others. He insists that we must strive to recognize the difference between our picture of another person, as it is narcissistically determined by our feelings about the person, and the person's reality as it truly exists beyond our needs.[30]

More recently, Robert Sternberg investigated the nature of love and its main components. In his article, "A Triangular Theory of Love," he presents a theory of love which includes three integral parts: intimacy, passion, and decision/commitment. The intimacy component refers to "feelings of closeness, connectedness, and bondedness...."Essentially, it is the experience of warmth in loving relationships and derived largely from emotional investment. The passion component refers to drives that "lead to romance, physical attraction, sexual consummation, and related phenomena in loving relationships." Essentially, the passion component is derived from motivational involvement. Finally, the decision/commitment component includes the "cognitive elements that are involved in decision-making about the existence of and potential long-term commitment to a loving relationship."[31]

Sternberg and Michael Barnes explain the relationship among the three components by referring to dissimilar triangles. An equilateral triangle represents a balanced love in which the three components are roughly balanced. Three unbalanced triangles represent an emphasis placed on one of the components over the others. For example, one triangle represents an emphasis on passion wherein physical attraction may play a large role while intimacy and commitment play smaller roles. Another triangle emphasizes intimacy wherein the lovers in the relationship may be good friends, but physical attraction and commitment to the future are not so strong. The last unbalanced triangle represents an emphasis on decision/commitment wherein intimacy or physical attraction has waned or never developed. The researchers suggest that by changing the shape of the triangles, it is possible to represent a wide variety of love relationships.

While the decision/commitment component relates directly to our discussion, the other components are equally important.[32] This component consists of two aspects, a short-term one (a decision that a certain one is loved), and a long-term one (a commitment to maintain that certain loved one).

It is important to note that a decision to love does not necessarily imply a commitment to love. For example, a person might make a decision to love another, but is unable to acknowledge a commitment. Sternberg points out that the institution of marriage represents a legalization of the decision to love. Hopefully, the commitment aspect will grow in the process of the marriage.[33]

Many times, intimacy and passion (the heat or charge components) are maintained by the decision/commitment to love. In most cases, the commitment to love follows upon the decision to love. "The course of the decision/commitment component of love over the duration of a close relationship depends in large part on the success of that relationship."[34] He suggests that in successful relationships, the level of commitment will increase over a long period and then gradually level off into long-term stability. Of course, this takes into account that even in good marriages, there will be ups and downs in the commitment level.

Of course, there are many examples of the decision to love. One of the most important is the decision to love in marriage. A successful marriage is one in which the decision to love has been an important part of the relationship. In this marriage there is a balance akin to the theory presented by Sternberg: intimacy, passion, and decision/commitment.

The decision to love and marriage

The decision/commitment to love is expressed in many forums and forms in human life. Nowhere, however, is it more characteristic and important than in the sacrament and institution of marriage. For when two people pronounce public vows, one to another, in the presence of the community, they express their desire to know the other at the deepest level which is possible for human beings. In fact, for many the implicit goal of marriage is to know God through the knowledge and the love for the other.

Marriage: a creation of love

A marriage is a deliberate decision to create something new, a new creation. It is like any worthwhile creation in that it comes from the heart and mind of the creator(s). There is intense preparation and commitment to the development of the creation. In many ways, it is like the artist who prepares the canvas to take the impression of his or her creative mind and heart. It is a creation of love. A marriage, like

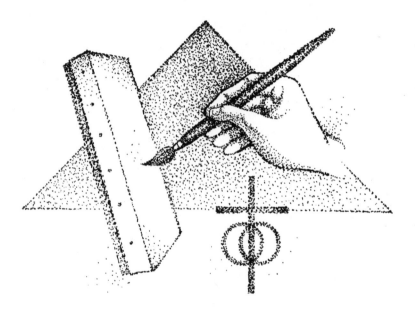

a painting, is a creation of love, one that takes attention, dedication, time and care to develop. In the end, the creation is pleasing for others to witness, experience, and meditate on. In the same way, a couple's creation in marriage, after many years, can be witnessed, experienced and meditated on. In a way, a couple paints a picture of their life together.

Painting a picture demands a series of decisions. First, it is inspired with a dream or an image of the painting. Second, the artist begins to sketch the outline of the painting, deciding almost automatically about color and form. In a burst of creativeness, unconscious images may come to conscious life in color and form. As each color is mixed with other colors, a new interpretation of life is expressed, the artist's interpretation of life. Each color or shape represents a decision emanating from the artist's soul, the artist's spirituality, if you will. His or her decisions become spiritual for they represent his or her very spirit of life, or way of viewing the world and, perhaps, the creator of all things. In a real way, there is a love relationship between the artist and the canvas on which appears his or her inner expression of creativeness. The artist seeks to express the beauty of creation in a visible form.

This metaphor of art can be applied to the creative love relationship in marriage. Two people who decide to marry are like artists who give life to a blank canvas. There is the attraction, then the development of a relationship. Dreams and images of life together come to life—dreams and images that live deep within their hearts, perhaps on the unconscious level. The dream of life begins to be created.

To paint, a gifted artist fills his or her palette with many colors from the universe. Married couples fill their palettes with the colors of life and share them with each other. These colors are not merely fragments of pigment and oil, but they are the values of life: mutual respect, trust, fidelity, honesty, genuineness, justice, generosity, gentleness, straightforwardness, and love. In their marriage, they skillfully choose many of the color values (virtues, values, and dreams) to bring to life the vision of marriage and family life, the seeds of which were present from early in the relationship.

So, when a couple first pronounces their marital vows, they take the blank canvas, primed with the grace of God, and add their emotional and physical heritage, the blessings of their family and friends, and make their first brush strokes on the marital canvas. These are usually broad strokes which outline the foundation on which they create their marital portrait.

Even as they make those first strokes, albeit with wide-eyed enthusiasm, they experience the uneven texture of life's canvas. The uneven texture which may be their personalities, their families of origin, religion, political and social culture, and unexpected challenges. Somehow they make a decision to pay more attention to some parts of their painting throughout marital life than others, for example, their personal values and cultural values. Those who decide to live a loving and responsible marital life are convinced that they will be able to meet every challenge with decisive attention to mutual concerns, good communication, mutual fidelity and trust, and patience and the acknowledgment of God's presence.

Of course, their marital portrait is always in progress. Just as it took some of the celebrated artists many years to paint a masterpiece, so it takes a couple many years to paint their marital portrait of love. To the casual observer, who sees the unfinished painting, it might appear to be merely a collage of day-to-day experiences—work, food shopping, cooking, little league games, babysitting, bills, etc. To the couple, however, each brush stroke, each decision, is meaningful. Each stroke holds its own beautiful story and enfolds into life, like a flower revealing its mysterious beauty through its color, texture, scent and shape. A small, insignificant part of the portrait, which might seem to others to be an unrelated incident, for them may be a focal and revelatory experience, something that stands out from all the rest. Only they know all that is attached to each moment and each decision. It is part of the mystery of love.

Even as they examine the unfinished portrait, they can reflect on how each of their daily contributions to the painting ultimately fits in. Certainly, they sometimes wonder how the portrait will look as it approaches completion in late adulthood. In the end, though, couples who sustain their decision to love will experience a fullness of life that was only a dream in the beginning of the relationship.

Marriage and sacrament

All the sacraments express the mysterious signs of God's love, the love that shapes our hearts and minds. In the celebration of the sacraments, many symbols of God's creative activity among us are used to reach the deep collective unconscious recesses of our psyche. Just after birth, children are washed in the living waters and then are sealed with the oils of life. They are made ready to live in a community of people who can expect the encouraging presence of the Spirit. Later in maturity, they are nourished with the bread of life, a basic sustenance for all cultures.

In marriage, the previous sacramental symbols are brought together as if in a symphony of symbols, a holy union of intentions, an unbreakable bond, a rainbow of colors. In marriage, the husband and wife renew their baptismal union with the entire people of God, renew their beliefs in Jesus' presence in the Holy Spirit, and nourish each other through the reception of the Lord's holy word and his body and blood. In a word, the two become the sacrament of God's presence because of their love for God and one another. They are the living sacrament, the sign of God's generous love in a world which needs signs of love so much.

Perhaps marital portraits give a deeper insight into God's love for each of us, just as the life of Jesus was an attempt to paint a living portrait of the Godhead among human beings. It is no wonder that so many artists and sculptors attempted to reproduce his portrait on canvas and stone. They may have wanted to capture the goodness of his life and share it with others.

Jesus' life portrait: a model for all

Jesus lived a simple life, some say, an insignificant life. The decisions of his life were not significant for the most part, but they were all informed with the desire to do the will of his Father. Each one was a spiritual one. Each was informed by a commitment to purpose (to reveal the Father's love to a people who had forgotten the meaning of love); a determination to do what is good; a consistent attitude of acceptance for all—Jew and Gentile, poor and rich, young and old, black and white; a committed willingness to preach God's message of love and forgiveness; and the development of a charitable heart even for his enemies.

In the end, Jesus' portrait reflected his decision to live for others. St. John described what Jesus said and did the best when he said, "Our love is not to be just words or mere talk, but something real and active; only by this can we be certain that we are children of the truth and be able to quiet our conscience in his presence..."(1 Jn 3:18). At the end of his life, Jesus reflected the presence of God.

Jesus' life is a model for us. We can imitate Jesus' pattern of decision-making by choosing to decide to reveal God's love for others; decide to do what is good; decide to accept others; decide to forgive; and decide to be of service. These basic decisions affect the decisions for a life.

As married couples paint their marital portrait,

perhaps the words of St. Paul to the Romans may help to explain their sentiments in marriage:

> Nothing can come between us and the love of Christ, even if we are troubled or worried, or being persecuted, or lacking food or clothes, or being threatened or even attacked.... These are the trials through which we triumph, by the power of him who loves us. For...neither death, nor life, no angel, no prince, nothing that exists,...or height or depth, nor any created thing, can ever come between us and the love of God made visible in Christ Jesus our Lord (Rom 8:35–39).

All of this came from the one decision to love, a spiritual decision. The greatest of all decisions is the decision to love, for it influences all the others. The decision to love does not stand alongside the other decisions of life. It is their model. Each decision becomes a spiritual one and we slowly discover that we are spiritual. ✗

* * *

The decision to love is a vital attitude. Once we decide to love, our whole being is involved with the other. It is a major part of the spirituality of life.

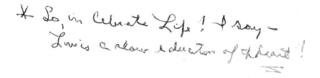

✗ So, in Celibate Life! I say — Love is a slow education of the heart!

Chapter Four
The Decision to Work

"What do I want to be when I grow up?"

This is the question that traditionally haunts high school and college students. In our time it is also a question that a growing number of adults ask—half jokingly, half seriously.

In a world and time where things were more fixed, stable and unchanging, it was assumed that a person made a choice early on in life about what his or her life's work would be. More often than not, the limits on the opportunities of one's social or economic standing determined the range of education or work possibilities.

Sometimes it was family tradition or the ownership of a small business that guided the decision for life and occupation.

All of that has changed! There are still many who make the choice for life's work and occupation once, acquire the needed education and training, and spend the rest of their lives plying their trade. However, a growing number of people find, by choice or by necessity of circumstances, that they make fundamental choices for work several times throughout the course of their lives. Changing technologies, the birth and death of businesses and institutions, mass layoffs and job retraining, growing freedom and mobility—these are just some of the circumstances that lead people in our day to ask again and again, "What do I want to be now? What work do I want to take up? Where can I make my greatest contribution and mark?"

It is not just the frequency of this question that has changed but the quality of the question of life work has changed too. In its crudest form, the question was and still is, "How can I make a living and support myself and family?" The question, as asked in our very different social circumstances, may also be, "What work is most needed in our time?" Witness the large number of young people who are attracted to environmental occupations. The question may be more vocational in tone, "What work do my gifts call me to?"

In this dramatically changed world of work and life choices for work, the spiritual nature of the decision to work becomes more obvious and more compelling. Our religious tradition has always acknowledged that some work choices had a spiritual density that was apparent. Especially those choices that steered people in the direction of a life dedicated to religious or church service were recognized as spiritual and called "vocations." On deeper analysis, the same spiritual forces at play in this "religious vocation" are at play in all serious choices about work. In order to capture some of the spiritual dimension in the decision to work, it is useful to reflect on two aspects of this decision: the sacredness of work and the sacredness of the choice.

The sacredness of work

The Judeo-Christian tradition decided very early on that productive human activity was not just work. It was much more. It was a participation in the very creative work of God. Read the book of Genesis on the creation of the world (Gen 1:1–2:25, especially 1:26–31). God not only created man and woman in his own image and likeness but he made them "masters" of the whole natural productive machinery of his creation—all of the creatures of the sea, the earth and sky, all of the things that grow upon the earth. The two traditions of the creation story in Genesis use slightly different imagery to communicate the responsibility to carry on the work of creation. The one tradition clearly sets Adam as "master" of the rest of creation: the second tradition, in more poetic and symbolic fashion, depicts "the man" as giving names to all of the creatures of the earth. In both cases, the intent is identical.

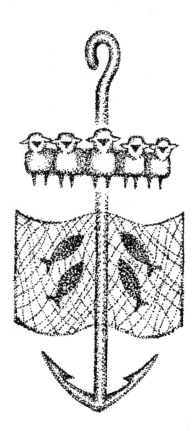

Sovereignty over the continuation of creation is transferred from divine to human hands. What was begun by God and was holy because it came from God was to continue and still be holy in the hands of man and woman.

Israel and its spiritual tradition maintained a profound sense of the sacredness of the earth and the particular sacredness of the work of human hands. One interesting aspect of the history of Israel and its attitude toward work and human labor is revealed in the way in which some professions are transformed from a purely "secular" endeavor into a more pastoral and sacred function. The profession of shepherding is a good case in point. The image of God as shepherd is deep in our religious consciousness. "The Lord is my shepherd" (Psalm 23) is one of the most fundamental and familiar of all prayers. The image of the leader of God's people as a shepherd is a tradition that leads eventually to the assertion of Jesus that he is "the good shepherd" (Jn 10:11). What is intriguing for this reflection on the sacredness of work is the way in which God used the practical work of shepherding as the preparation for so many of the early leaders of his people. Abraham, Moses and David were all practicing shepherds before they were called to lead God's flock. There was something in the nature of shepherding that prepared its practitioners to stand in God's place as the head of his people.

This transition and transformation of word from the secular to the sacred is the same instinct that led Jesus to invite Simon and his brother Andrew who were at the time carrying on the very business of casting nets to "Follow me and I will make you fishers of men" (Mk 1:16–17).

Human work provided more than a series of good images to communicate the presence of God in the community leadership. St. Paul and all subsequent Christian tradition views the carrying out of human endeavors as an act of building up the body of Christ. In the letter to the Ephesians, that most spiritual of the summaries of the teaching of Paul, the author states explicitly that the human functions of teaching, administrating, evangelizing, all constitute together "a unity in the work of service, building up the body of Christ" (Eph 4:13). The work of human hands can create the very presence of Christ in the community.

Reflecting on this scriptural tradition about human labor and its sacredness is a sobering reminder of how often we underestimate and underesteem our human activity. Our natural instinct is to think of work in the terms of that other scriptural tradition that sees human labor as a curse, the result of the infidelity of our first parents (Gen 2:17–19). What makes this attitude about work so easy to assume is the fact that much of our work is drudgery. Fatigue or boredom are, realistically, the natural companions or outcomes of much of human labor.

Yet, when we are able to see our work as a part of something larger, a vast complex pattern through which the world is becoming what it should be, then our small or large contribution through work takes on a level of meaning that can be described only as spiritual and sacred. Human labor is holy. When we work with seriousness, dedication and all of the competence we can muster, we are changing the world and are inching it toward what it can be in its best expression.

The sacredness of the choice

If what you do for a living is in reality a participation in the creative transformation of the world, if your work is a continuation of God's work, then the way you choose or rechoose your life work has a sacred dimension to it. The choice becomes sacred when you realize you are not just choosing a career but a vocation.

It has already been asserted that all of the spiritual forces at play in a "religious vocation" are at play in all serious choices about work. Again, scripture is the first place to look to identify what some of these spiritual forces are.

Almost all of the key figures in both the Hebrew and the Christian scriptures who transform the life of God's people in various roles come to those roles through a clear consciousness of being called by God. Leaders, prophets, apostles—all are acutely aware that they are doing God's work because they were called to do so by God. Some of the most poignant, the most intimate, the most touching moments in the scriptures occur when God is calling one of his own. The calls of Samuel, the last of the Judges, Isaiah, the greatest of the prophets, and Mary, the first of the Christian saints, have striking similarities.

Samuel was a young boy in service to the priest Eli at the Shiloh, the shrine of the Lord. He was the miracle child given to his parents after years of barrenness and given by his parents, in turn, to the service of their God. One night when Samuel was asleep in the sanctuary of the Lord, he heard a voice call repeatedly, "Samuel, Samuel." He wakened his master, the priest Eli, several times and Eli, recognizing the source of the voice, told Samuel to respond the next time it called, "Speak, Lord, your servant is listening." The Lord spoke to Samuel again and again throughout his long life, a life that helped move Israel from tribe to nation.

The lesson for the young Samuel, the lesson for all who are open to the call of God, is that the voice of God is not always easily recognizable. Hearing it the first time can be confusing. But the prayer of Samuel stands forever as the only effective prayer for those who wish to hear, "Speak, Lord, your servant is listening."

Isaiah was far from being an innocent lad without experience. From the evidence scattered throughout the books of his prophecy, he was a man of political influence, and not a totally virtuous man at that. His call recorded in Isaiah, chapter 6, catches him by surprise. It is not a subtle voice but a stunning vision of the mastery of God in the sanctuary. Isaiah's first reaction is to shrink back, fully conscious of the deceitfulness of his own lips, being among a people of unclean lips. His lips are seared by the hot coal borne to him by the seraph and his sense of sinfulness is dispelled. When the voice of the Lord says,

"Whom shall I send?" Isaiah's cleansed lips part and he responds, "Here I am, send me."

The often unspoken assumption about God's call is that it comes to the good and the innocent, the talented and the prepared. Sacred history, and certainly the image of Isaiah, should convince us that the one necessary ingredient of a call to do God's work is not prior virtue but current willingness—"Here I am, send me."

The young Mary in the early chapters of Luke's gospel offers another response to an unexpected, unanticipated and confusing call. The angel Gabriel appeared to her and proclaimed her "blessed." When told that she will bear a son to rule from David's throne, she moved from confusion to questioning, "How can this be?" and finally to submission, "Let what you have said be done to me." The overpowering sense that this was not all of her doing and not in her hands and control led Mary to the point of letting go. Some larger work, some God-inspired plan was in the making and her true response could only be, "Let it be."

> Speak, Lord!
> Here I am!
> Let it be!

Three powerful responses to the experience of being called: three normal people at very different points in their lives, none of them expecting to hear the voice of God; three images that support the realization that this is the way God works with all who are open to hearing the call. The work to be done is always unique to the individual. The spirit in which it is done is the same, the deep conviction that in faith God can work through us.

*   *   *

Making a choice for a life's work or even mulling over the options for work or service that lie before us is a sacred moment. It is one of those unique moments in life in which we can be sure that God is near. In chapter six, The Decision to Serve, several examples are given that exemplify the decision to choose a work as a sacred experience.

Chapter Five

The Decision to Endure

*S*piritual wisdom comes at times from unexpected quarters. A column on the sports page of a large east coast city newspaper made a case for the value of a particular pitcher to the local major league baseball team. The pitcher, a seasoned veteran, had had a few brilliant seasons but was in a bad slump. He suffered the indignity of being taken out of the starting pitching rotation and was made to sit on the bench as a relief pitcher. The columnist made a case for his value to the team as a man who knew how to cope with failure and endure in spite of setbacks. He held him up as a model for younger players in a sport that usually only recognizes winners and seldom reflects on the value of graceful losers.

Anyone who is able to endure setbacks with grace, who can maintain inner composure and dignity in failure, is not a bad model for all. The existence of such a person illustrates the point that endurance—the ability to cope with sustained pressure, pain, or failure—can spring from a deep spiritual foundation.

The decision to endure the difficulties that life hands us is at the heart of the Christian tradition. The symbol that sits at the center of the Christian tradition is the symbol of the cross. In fact, the cross was originally the symbol of ignominy and failure. To take an instrument of public execution and to transform it into a symbol of triumph speaks volumes about our conviction that sustained pressure, pain, or failure can be transformed into something life-giving.

Our own age seems to have ambivalent feelings about endurance; it both admires and avoids it. Television is full of examples of contrived endurance—marathons, races, survival camps, blind sailors who want to cross the Atlantic alone. All harbor a sense of admiration for someone who submits to painful and demanding circumstances and in the end is able to overcome. At the same time, however, people who are struggling with failed relationships or difficult work situations are not readily affirmed by others, even their friends.

To affirm the spiritual nature of the decision to endure requires that two extremes are avoided. The first

extreme is the very dour, pessimistic attitude of some puri-
tanical Christians that human suffering is the only thing
that has spiritual meaning and that it constitutes God's
way of keeping the world straight. Since all are sinners, the
only thing that is deserved is adversity. Therefore, it can be
interpreted as the only road to salvation. The opposite
extreme is to see no value or point to human suffering and
endurance. It ought to be avoided at all costs and it has no
spiritual dimension. The resurrection completely obscures
the cross; joy is to be celebrated, pain denied.

The endurance of Jesus

One of the most instructive ways to read the story
of Jesus as presented in the synoptic gospels is to see Jesus
as the rabbi giving intense and prolonged instructions to
his disciples on the meaning and working of the kingdom.
Of all of the lessons that Jesus taught, the most difficult
was that he must go to Jerusalem and to suffer and die
there at the hands of religious leaders (Mt 16:21; Mk 8:31;
Lk 9:22). As Matthew and Mark tell the story of this first
prediction of the passion, Peter tries to correct this mis-
guided death wish of the rabbi and he attempts to take
him aside and dismiss the notion. There are not many
instances in the gospel where Jesus is as harsh and direct
in rebuking one of his own. He said, "Get behind me,
Satan!" The one who was shortly before designated as
"Rock" now becomes a stumbling block, an insidious
entrapment to Jesus, standing in his way of accepting the
suffering that will be his. Just to make sure that the disci-

ples understand the road that discipleship will lead them on, Jesus says that anyone who wants to follow him must be as willing as he to accept the cross. "If anyone wants to be a follower of mine, let him renounce himself and take up his cross and follow me" (Mt 16:24).

Jesus is absolutely unflinching and uncompromising in his determination to face this painful fate. He will go through and not around his suffering. His conviction and motivation are that true life—resurrected life—comes only by the endurance of suffering. His strength is not that of the stoic who believes in the natural virtue of suffering and endurance. His strength is that of the person who believes in God and the purposefulness of all human experience, including suffering.

Endurance: not just survival

As mentioned already, Robert Jay Lifton[35] believes in the resiliency of the human person. The person who possesses a "Protean Self" is able to endure and not merely survive.

Thinking of enduring suffering, even in the spirit of Jesus, often evokes an image of an individual locked into grim, stolid perseverance, just hanging on in the face of life's toughest punishments. Endurance of the spirit is more than just surviving or hanging on until the worst is over. It is more than the conviction that suffering will end. It is the conviction that suffering has a purpose. It is the experience of endurance itself as a pilgrimage, as a passage to a deeper wisdom and a deeper grasp of the mystery of human existence.

In the traditional literature on the spiritual life, the benefit of endurance that leads to a deeper spiritual life is found in the notion of "purgation." Purgation is a process of stripping away all that is evil, all that is non-essential, all that impedes the growth of the spirit. Purgation is a passive process. It is the will to let some part of us die. In the classic treatment of passive purgation, "The Dark Night," St. John of the Cross reminds spiritual seekers that the dark night affects the senses and the spirit as well. In fact, it is only in the deepest night of spiritual abandonment by God that God is truly encountered. Endurance can lead one to this perfectly inexplicable irony in the spiritual life. When we feel most abandoned by God, we are, in fact, most intimate.

The spiritual reality of purgation helps us to cope with and give meaning to the most difficult aspect of living with endurance—the sense of personal loss. Putting up with and living through the setbacks and pains of life inevitably leave us with the feeling that we have been cheated by life. It doesn't take much to find someone who appears to be much better off than we are, usually someone judged to be less deserving. So, if God is fair and just, why should one suffer loss while others prosper?

Endurance of the spirit and its consequent stripping away of non-essentials helps us to see our loss in a different light. It can be experienced as a process of lightening our load, setting aside the impediments to a genuinely full life. Another dynamic of the decision to endure in the spirit is the discovery that people do survive. It is never quite clear where the strength comes from, but there is a strong suspicion that it is a gift of God, an extraordinary moment of grace not attributable to our normal abilities.

Endurance: a common grace

One helpful way to bring us to a decision to endure is to be open to the many examples of genuine graced endurance that exist all around us. Every community, every neighborhood, every church congregation is replete with stories of individuals and families who have demonstrated everything from commendable courage to extraordinary heroism. What is a common thread in many of these stories of graced endurance is a simplicity, an unassuming attitude on the part of those who endured that this is just what had to be done. They see nothing extraordinary in what they are doing. It is those of us who are witness to their strength, often their heroism, that see the extraordinary nature of their actions.

There is a priest who tells the story of a young girl in his parish who waged a long and seemingly successful battle with cancer. The priest had spent many hours with the family and stood in absolute admiration of the parents' and child's courage and endurance. A year or so after her last hospital stay, the child asked her mother one day, "What do you see when you look into God's eyes?" The mother decided that that type of question was the priest's department, so she passed it on to him. After some reflection, the priest remembered where he had last come close to seeing God's eyes, and he responded to the little girl that if she wanted to see what was in God's eyes, she should look into the mirror. Those who endure in grace and in the spirit do become icons for us, a window into the world of the truly spiritual.

*   *   *

The decision to endure whatever it is that life hands us does not preclude the possibility of changing our actions. It doesn't eliminate the possibility that what we must face is really beyond us. It does offer one spiritually significant way to respond to God. It is a decision to wait and be still. It is a decision to be found. It is a difficult decision.

Chapter Six
The Decision to Serve

"*S he would never look down on people. She would always appreciate what people were worth, and it didn't matter whether they were poor or whatever.*"

"He taught me never to forget where you came from; to always appreciate anything from anybody. Be honest and straightforward. See other people as your friends. All people are people."[36]

"God calls to us many times in our life. We do not always hear him. But sometimes, when we least expect it, he touches us deeply and profoundly. If we are very fortunate, it is at these moments that we stop, think, and pray. Then we can decide to try to answer

God's call." These words were spoken by a modern day helper.[37]

The "feeling of effort" for ministry

Faith and service (ministry) should be linked in our cultural experience, especially in religious culture. Both reflect a specific choice or decision on the part of an individual or group to put the rights and needs of others—what we term respect—before any other good, even one's own. A Jewish person rescued by a Christian said of the rescuer's motivation: "They were performing a great deed without any ulterior motives, and their goodness was truly rare. I constantly had evidence of their kindness, and I know that it stemmed largely from their deep faith."[38]

This chapter will focus on two true-to-life examples of service. It is evident that in these examples the people were deeply moved, in specific ways, to share their lives with others. Their decisions for service were spiritually based, as evidenced by their commitment over a long period of time, even when faced with adversity. They possess a spirit of life which filters their human experiences.

In a previous chapter, we discussed the decision to love as the foundational point of all values in life. Love moves us to action or some type of service. For as we heard from St. Paul, the word of the Lord specifically demands that any intent or feeling without action is only half the work of the Christian. The decision to serve is intimately connected to the decision to love. It reflects a spirituality of care for others which is reflected in all decisions.

The decision to serve flows from the decisions to believe and love. For those who choose to decide for service, many of their decisions become spiritual. In a very real way, their view of God, the world, self, and others is dramatically influenced. They discover a new way of life.

Love and service are found in the language and practice (theory and action) of both secular and religious spheres since they seem to capture the essence of what it means to be fully human. In fact, the foundation of many religious movements and institutions is based on these two principles: to love God and serve one's neighbor. These are the vertical (to the transcendent or Holy One) and horizontal aspects (to other human beings) of human relationships. The authors of many democratic constitutions have based their ideas on the decisions for love of God and service of neighbor as the hallmarks of human values.

The revelation of love and service is most clearly shown when people find themselves in crises, such as natural disasters: for example, the floods in Pennsylvania, in Florida, and in the Midwest; the earthquakes in California and Japan; the volcanic eruptions in Oregon, Hawaii, and Japan; world wars and international conflicts. As a result of these crises, many do seem to serve another.

The true test is whether similar behaviors continue over a longer period of time after the crises are over. By themselves, then, crises do not increase people's positive social behaviors. The spirituality of an individual must be the filter through which experience must pass.

The impulse to serve: caring

The internal impulses to serve others emanate from the values of caring—the need to be helpful, hospitable, concerned, empathic and loving. Jesus asked his followers to live the values of caring. He asked them, above all, to be models of faith and service. Service cannot be understood without specific examples, so what follows are two examples of altruistic service.

Rescuers of those condemned: an example of caring

In a magnificent study which supported the reality of an altruistic personality trait, Paul and Pearl Oliner studied the values of caring found in the rescuers of Jews. Many of the rescuers attributed the source of those values to the values they learned from parents, such as, "I learned to live honestly,...to respect others, and to have compassion and generosity toward those who were less well treated by life."[39]

Oliner and Oliner also pointed out that a major characteristic of the rescuers' personalities was their ethical values. These values were nurtured since childhood. For example, while growing up, rescuers were not influenced by distinctions of class and religion in the choice of friends. "They were not only more likely to befriend Christians of other denominations but were also significantly more likely to befriend Jews that were bystanders."[40] This attitude extended into adulthood.

These rescuers exhibited a sense of competence. Their decisions were fueled by a "feeling of effort" or will, not because of conformity, compliance or coercion. This sense of competence, when coupled with an ability to care and respect others, could explain why the rescuers chose to help others. In a very real way, their entire life was a preparation, each decision based on a caring and faith-filled spirituality for the decision to serve, even if it meant the loss of their life.

"My Brother's Keeper": an example of care

The stories and personalities of modern-day rescuers are not too different from the rescuers described by Oliner and Oliner. What follows is a story of an ordinary man and woman, Jim and Terry, who, after making a Cursillo retreat, made the decision to serve. They decided to serve the needs of the poor based on their interpretation of God's call to serve the poor. In a very real way, they are an example of a new breed of Christian lay people who are giving their entire lives in service to others.

Their ministry was born from a simple idea: to help satisfy the material needs of the poor. They decided to serve others by collecting furniture (and other items needed for a home) from donors, repairing the articles, and giving them to the poor. They, and their many follow-ers (religious, clergy and lay people—all volunteers without pay), use trucks to pick up the donated material, enhance it, and then deliver it to the needy. The program is called "My Brother's Keeper."[41]

Jim and Terry are ordinary people. He is a man who worked his entire life in the service of others, as a union organizer fighting for member rights, and a counselor to the mentally handicapped. He reported that he always felt competent at any task that he undertook. Presently, because of the demands of "My Brother's Keeper," he works part-time as a counselor and the rest of the week and weekends, at the service center. Terry, a vibrant and energetic mother of three children, is a secretary part-time and a full-time co-director at "My Brother's Keeper." No one receives a salary—including the founders, Jim and Terry.

How did it all happen for this couple? One evening, Jim and Terry were watching a movie, "God Bless the Child," which is a true story about a homeless mother and her seven-year-old daughter. The mother voluntarily decided to give up her child because she could not adequately take care of her.

Jim said this about their decision to serve:

> One night we sat in the kitchen and talked. We did not want this to be just another movie, one more TV special or tragic news story that we could put out of our minds as we started our everyday business the next morning. We wanted to help in some way that made a difference. We had no idea what it might be. We felt that we had to make a commitment at that moment to do something. So, we went into the bedroom, stood holding hands in front of the crucifix and talked to the Lord Jesus. We asked Christ to use us to

help people. We made a covenant: if he would use us to serve people in his name and put the work in front of us, then we would make ourselves available and put his work first. So the journey began.[42]

From the very start, they decided that this would be a work of God. So they committed themselves to some basic guidelines. They would not allow their names to be used in any way. In fact, the name of the project was only placed in small letters on the doors of the trucks in compliance with state law. They also promised not to allow any monetary donations to build up in the bank. As soon as the amount would grow beyond that needed for daily expenses, it would be spent to buy articles for the needy. Since no money is used for salaries, those who serve are all volunteers in the true sense of the word.

As with the development of any volunteer service, it was difficult to get it in action. What follows is just a little taste of how it all happened. After deciding to serve, Jim and Terry made up some flyers which asked for clothing for the needy. Jim confessed, "It did not occur to us then that we did not know anyone in need although we were both needy at one time." Before they knew it, they were receiving many bags of usable clothes. They spent their evenings sorting, cleaning, and folding clothing while watching TV. The story continues.

During the first four years, "My Brother's Keeper" grew by leaps and bounds. Even other established

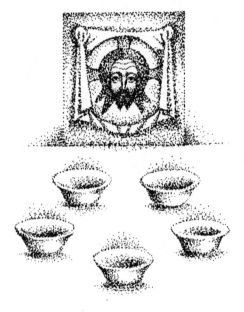

service agencies began to call Jim and Terry for their services for those who could not find help through the normal system.[43]

Jim tells a story about a "miracle" when ministering to one family in Dorchester, Massachusetts. The first truck (the Green Bomb) that Jim was using broke down on the way to this delivery. He had spoken many times to the person in need, Marilyn, and she was waiting for the help. Jim did not want to disappoint her or her children. While Jim was trying to get repairs, another trucker offered assistance. Since Jim's vehicle was not able to be revived that day (or ever), the stranger took Jim's truck on one of his flatbed trucks with all the furniture to their destination. When they arrived Marilyn and the children were waiting outside.

Jim told the rest of the story this way:

> Before bringing any furniture in, I went up to check out the apartment to determine which furniture would be going in what rooms. The place was completely empty except for blankets on the floor in the various rooms. When I got to the kitchen, there were five bowls of soup sitting on the floor. They were in an almost perfect circle. We brought in the beds and pullout couches and small tables and lamps. The last thing to come up was the kitchen table and chairs. When the table was assembled, we picked the bowls of soup up

from the floor and set them on it. Then I handed Marilyn a picture of Jesus and said, "We're just the delivery men, this is the person who sent you the furniture." Her face came alive and she embraced each of us.[44]

Incredible things happened in just a few years. Jim and Terry saw mothers with children sleeping on hard and damp floors; families living without refrigerators; and parents in need of food to feed their families.

Jim, himself, had come from a life of poverty as a child. He remarked that "For a long time, in my adult years, I had been insulated from poverty." He went on to say that "I had forgotten how scared I was at eight, when my older brother had killed the mother rat who had leaped at him in our kitchen."

This service to the community has grown extensively. After five years "My Brother's Keeper" uses three delivery trucks (all donated) and has over fifty active volunteers (with hundreds who assist in special projects). They have serviced thousands of people and have opened the hearts of many around them.

Their Brother's Keeper prayer summarizes the ministry. It says, "Lord when I experience the joy of giving to my children help me to remember the agony of those who must watch their children go without." In another part, it says, "By remembering, help me to destroy my indifference and arouse my compassion. Make me concerned enough to act in your name, to help those who cry out to you for that which I so often take for granted."

The story of "My Brother's Keeper" is only one among thousands of stories that can be told about caring people who decide to serve. It is a "type five decision," in William James' terminology, one that entails willfulness or a "feeling of effort."

*   *   *

The decision to serve flows out of a spirit of life which is characterized by a decision to believe, a decision to love, a decision to work, and a decision to endure. The decision to serve expresses each person's spiritual self in a very vivid way.

Conclusion

*T*his book has explored the relationship between decision-making and the spiritual life. Basically, the scriptures suggest that the spiritual life is based on a response to the Spirit of Life. When a person chooses Jesus as a model for a way of life, he or she makes a decision to live a spirit of life or a spirituality. As a consequence, all decisions are then informed by a spirituality based on the message of Jesus in the Spirit.

In the development of a spirituality or a spirit of life, a person participates in a process of formation, informed by the Spirit. In this process, it is important for the person to stay awake and to be willing to be open to experience. Slowly, in the process of spiritual formation, the person begins to view, cope, and act in the world in a way that is in accord with the Spirit of Life. The heart begins to express ideas that are challenging both to the person and to others who experience the person.

The spirituality that the heart speaks is unique to the individual. So as decisions are made, they are filtered through the Spirit of Life that informs the person's identity. Spirituality slowly becomes a daily way of living—a way of viewing and interpreting life in the present; a vision for life that emphasizes the spiritual life; a way of believing that makes sense; a filter through which to decide about faith, love, work, endurance, and service.

William James suggests that important decisions in life involved a "feeling of effort." These types of decisions involve both reason and the creative contributions of the spirit. With every deliberate choice, "an excursion into a lonesome moral wilderness" is made. This excursion is based on the decision to believe. As it was for the author Kazantzakis, the decision to believe is a lifelong process, with greater and greater refinements to assent. As James points out, there is no doubting the fact that our belief system affects thinking, and, ultimately, behavior. However, once the presence of God becomes a reality in the belief system, life is changed forever.

The decision to believe is a spiritual act, a real act of the will, and not merely a conception formed by the imagination of others. What follows this major decision are the other important decisions which characterize the

spiritual personality. The decision to love establishes the basis for all growing relationships. The decision to work allows participation in the very creative work of God. The decision to endure offers a significant way to respond to God, a decision to wait and be still. Finally, the decision to serve offers a way to express faith, hope, and love. The major decisions, which in turn affect many of our day-to-day decisions, are an expression of each person's unique spirituality.

*　*　*

In the end, the stuff of living a healthy spiritual life is the stuff of developing a spirituality. As the Spirit of Life in Jesus is accepted, daily decisions become informed with a new view of self, others, and the world.

Notes

1. *Jerusalem Bible* (Garden City, NY: Doubleday, 1966), p. 279. All scriptural quotes are taken from the *Jerusalem Bible*.

2. Joseph Fitzmyer, *Romans* (Garden City, NY: Doubleday, 1993), p. 488.

3. Bernard McGinn, "The Letter and the Spirit: Spirituality as an Academic Discipline," *The Cresset*, June 1993, p. 13.

4. Ibid., p. 17.

5. John Garvey, "Spirituality Made Simple: Just Stay Awake," *America*, October, 1990, Vol. 26, p. 601.

6. Gerald Broccolo, *Vital Spiritualities: Naming the Holy in Your Life* (Notre Dame, IN: Ave Maria Press, 1990), p. 13.

7. Martin Buber, "Heart Searching and the Particular Way," in *Modern Spirituality*, edited by John Garvey (Springfield, IL: Templegate Publishers, 1985), p. 4.

8. Ibid., p. 5.

9. William James, *The Varieties of Religious Experience* (New York: Collier, 1961), p. 52.

10. Ibid., p. 59.

11. *Boston Globe*, July 20, 1993.

12. Robert J. Lifton, *The Protean Self: Human Resilience in an Age of Fragmentation* (New York: Basic Books, 1993), p. 1.

13. William James, *The Principles of Psychology* (New York: Henry Holt, 1913), Vol. 11, ch. XXVI.

14. Samuel P. Oliner & Pearl M. Oliner, *The Altruistic Personality: Rescuers of Jews in Nazi Europe* (New York: The Free Press, 1988).

15. John Darley & Bibb Latané, "Bystanders' Intervention in Emergencies: Diffusion of Responsibility," *Journal of Personality and Social Psychology*, Vol. 8, 1968.

16. James, 1913, p. 534.

17. Andrew Garrod (Ed.), *Approaches to Moral Development* (New York: Teachers College Press, 1993), p. ix.

18. Nikos Kazantzakis, *The Saviors of God: Spiritual Exercises* (New York: Touchstone Books, 1960), p. 51.

19. Ibid., pp. 51–52.

20. Erik H. Erikson, *Childhood and Society*, 2nd ed. (New York: Norton, 1961), p. 268.

21. James, *The Principles of Psychology*, Vol. 1, p. 181.

22. The psychological communities' recent re-newed interest in the ideas of William James may suggest a reexamination of the long-lived and exclusive mechanistic

---

explanation of the human person. See Margaret E. Donnelly, ed., *Reinterpreting the Legacy of William James* (Washington, DC: American Psychological Association, 1992).

23. James, *The Varieties of Religious Experience*, p. 59.

24. Ibid., p. 71.

25. Ibid., p. 72.

26. Ibid., p. 72.

27. James Hillman, *The Thought of the Heart and the Soul of the World* (Dallas, TX: Spring, 1992).

28. Paul Tillich, *What Is Religion?* (New York: Harper Torchbooks, 1973), p. 67.

29. William James, *The Varieties of Religious Experience: A Study of Human Nature* (New York: Collier Books, 1961), p. 73.

30. Erich Fromm, *The Art of Loving* (New York: Harper and Row, 1956).

31. Robert Sternberg, "A Triangular Theory of Love," *Psychological Review*, Vol. 93, p. 119.

32. See Robert J. Sternberg and Michael L. Barnes, *The Psychology of Love* (New Haven, CT: Yale University Press, 1988) for a more detailed explanation.

33. Sternberg, "A Triangular Theory of Love."

34. Ibid., p. 127.

35. Robert Jay Lifton, *The Protean Self: Human Resilience in an Age of Fragmentation* (New York: Basic Books).

36. Samuel P. Oliner & Pearl M. Oliner, *The*

Altruistic Personality: Rescuers of Jews in Nazi Europe (New York: The Free Press, 1988), p. 143. (These sentiments were spoken by a young, Christian, seventeen-year-old who risked his life to save persecuted Jews from death. He attributed his altruistic behavior to his parents' influence on him.)

37. *Notes from "My Brother's Keeper."* From James Orcutt, *Notes on My Brother's Keeper* (Unpublished notes, 1993).

38. Oliner & Oliner, 1988, p. 154.

39. Ibid., p. 164.

40. Ibid., p. 176.

41. The program is located in Brockton, Massachusetts.

42. *Notes from "My Brother's Keeper."*

43. Ibid.

44. Ibid.

References

Broccolo, G. T. (1990). *Vital Spiritualities: Naming the Holy in Your Life*. Notre Dame, IN: Ave Maria Press.

Buber, M. (1985) "Heart Searching and the Particular Way," in *Modern Spirituality*. Edited by John Garvey, pp. 1–7. Springfield, IL: Templegate Publishers.

Darley, J. and Latané, B. (1968). "Bystanders' Intervention in Emergencies: Diffusion of Responsibility." *Journal of Personality and Social Psychology* Vol. 8, pp. 377–383.

Donnelly, M. E. (Ed.). (1992). *Reinterpreting the Legacy of William James*. Washington, DC: American Psychological Association.

Erikson, E. H. (1961). *Childhood and Society* (2nd ed.). New York: Norton and Company.

Fitzmyer, J. (1993). *Romans*. The Anchor Bible Series. Vol. 33. New York: Doubleday.

Fromm, E. (1956). *The Art of Loving.* New York: Harper and Row.

Garrod, A. (Ed.) (1993). *Approaches to Moral Development: New Research and Emerging Themes.* New York: Teachers College Press.

Garvey, J. (October 1990). "Spirituality Made Simple: Just Stay Awake," *America,* 26, pp. 601–602.

Hillman, J. (1992). *The Thought of the Heart and the Soul of the World.* Dallas, TX: Spring.

James, W. (1913). *The Principles of Psychology.* Vol 1. New York: Henry Holt and Company.

—— (1913). *The Principles of Psychology.* Vol. 11. New York: Henry Holt and Company.

—— (1961). *The Varieties of Religious Experience: A Study of Human* Nature. New York: Collier Books.

Kazantzakis, N. (1960). *The Saviors of God: Spiritual Exercises.* New York: Touchstone Books.

Lifton, R. J. (1993). *The Protean Self: Human Resilience in an Age of Fragmentation.* New York: Basic Books.

McGinn, B. (June 1993). "The Letter and the Spirit: Spirituality as an Academic Discipline." *The Cresset,* pp. 13–22.

Oliner, S. P., & Oliner, P. M. (1988). *The Altruistic Personality: Rescuers of Jews in Nazi Europe.* New York: The Free Press.

Orcutt, J. (1993). *Notes on My Brother's Keeper.* Unpublished notes.

Sternberg, R. (1986). *A Triangular Theory of Love. Psychological Review,* Vol. 93, pp. 119–135.

Sternberg, R., and Barnes, M. L. (1988). (Eds.). *The Psychology of Love*. New Haven, CT: Yale University Press.

Tillich, P. (1948). *The Shaking of the Foundations*. New York: Scribner.

—— (1973). *What Is Religion?* New York: Harper Torchbooks.

ILLUMINATIONBOOKS

Other Books in the Series

Little Pieces of Light...Darkness and Personal Growth
by Joyce Rupp

Lessons from the Monastery That Touch Your Life
by M. Basil Pennington, O.C.S.O.

As You and the Abused Person Journey Together
by Sharon E. Cheston

Spirituality, Stress & You
by Thomas E. Rodgerson

Joy, The Dancing Spirit of Love Surrounding You
by Beverly Elaine Eanes

Why Are You Worrying?
by Joseph W. Ciarrocchi

Celebrating the Woman You Are
by S. Suzanne Mayer, I.H.M.